Elves for Beginners

Experiences, Conclusions, Healings and Elf-Gods

Contact: www.HarryEilenstein.de
Harry.Eilenstein@web.de
Harry Eilenstein at youtube

Production and publishing house: BoD - Books on Demand, Norderstedt

ISBN: 9783753454306

Table of Contents

I Elves?

What do elves have to do with serious magic? These lovely flower spirits from romantic stories and from fairy tales are not exactly what most magicians care about seriously and in detail – and hardly any other sensible person either.

The usual depiction of elves are small children or young women with butterfly wings – such beings do not seem to be a part of reality …

After all, the known elf depictions from the books of Cicely Mary Barker are very much based on the appearance of the respective plants, so that the elves appear as humanoid variants of the plants in question, so to speak.

But maybe a grain of truth can be found in the imaginative representations in the myths, legends and fairy tales. Let's see …

II   The history of the elves

II 1.   The word "elves"

It is almost always helpful to look at the history of the name and designation of a thing, if one wants to understand it better.

The word "Elves, Alben, Alfen, Elfen, Elben" comes from the Old Norse „alb" and describes there a group of spirits. The word itself is related to the Latin "albus" for "bright, white".

With these Albs the spirits of the dead are meant, as among other things the title "Alberich" ("king of albs") of the former North Germanic sungod, fathergod and god of the dead Tyr shows. This interpretation is also confirmed by the fact that the albs live in hills – these are the barrows where the dead rest.

The designation of the spirits of the dead as "white" or "bright" has two reasons: on the one hand, spirits of the dead can be perceived clairvoyantly as milky-white shadows with a slight blue shimmer, and on the other hand, the afterlife of the Germanic peoples lay in one of their afterlife concepts up in the sky in the bright ("white"), golden hall of the sungod-godfather Tyr. Therefore also Tyr himself was called "the white god".

However, since the Germanic tribes also had the burial chamber in the barrow and the simple burial in the earth, the albs began to be distinguished according to their place of residence as the "light albs" above in the sky and the „dark albs" in the barrows.

II 2.   Light elves and dark elves

From this distinction according to the place of residence of the ancestral spirits, which originated with the Germanic tribes, J.R.R. Tolkien created the Elves (light elves) and the Orcs (dark elves). Tolkien, who had been a professor of English at Oxford and had studied Germanic mythology intensively, brought the flower elf image, which was common in his time, back somewhat closer to the original Germanic image.

Tolkien's drastic-romantic depictions of the elves are rooted in his horoscope: He had a conjunction of Pluto ("drastic") and Neptune ("romantic") in the first house of his horoscope.

II 3.   Plant elves

The spirits in the barrows have already become "spirits on the barrows" among the Teutons – especially the sungod-godfather Tyr, reborn in the morning, sits on his barrow.

These "spirits on the barrows" have apparently become associated with the "plants on the barrows".

In the Germanic mythology also the first two humans were created from trees, thus from plants – and humans were very often described by the Teutons and also by the Celts as "beech of the sword" (man), "birch of the collar" (woman) and similar.

Probably by these associations then in the course of time the motive of the plant spirits developed.

Among the Teutons themselves the plant elf motif is still unknown.

II 4.   Erotic elves

The common erotic-feminine representation of the elves shows another root of this motif: In the Germanic myths, the earth and afterlife goddess unites with the dead man in the barrow, so that the dead man can beget himself, whereupon the goddess then gives birth to the dead man nine months later – the barrow is the belly of the earth goddess, who is pregnant with the re-begotten dead man. The seducing elves, who are almost always female, are the earth and afterlife goddess as the beautiful re-conception mistress of the dead.

Since the dead in their burial mounds were imagined as snakes and dragons, after all sorts of reinterpretations, the motif of the hero (dead man) developed, who climbs into a cave (burial chamber in the burial mound), kills the dragon (spirit of the dead) and frees the fair maiden (goddess of the afterlife) and then unites with her (re-conception).

II 5.   Fantasy images

Since these elf-imaginings are only the result of associations and not of experiences, experiments, observations and conclusions, they are a pure fiction, nothing else than a figment of human imagination – nowadays mainly an idealizing, romantic and partly very sweet and erotic image of seductive young women with butterfly wings.

III   Research on Elves

III 1.   Research principles

In view of this mythological-fantastic origin of today's elf conceptions, taking the elves seriously looks almost ridiculous – unless one sees them simply as reinterpreted and misunderstood ancestral spirits.

However, the conclusion that no conception whose origin can be explained from mythological images can have a reality content is somewhat rash. With this argumentation one could also reject the reincarnation, because this originated from the cycle of agriculture with the sowing, the growing, the harvest and the reseeding of the grain.

If one really wants to be sure (which is generally preferable to hasty conclusions), one must examine the thing itself about which one wants to know something – and not only the history of the ideas connected with this thing.

III 2.   A Working Hypothesis

Every verification needs a working hypothesis, and every experiment needs an approach from which to design an experimental setup. This approach can be very complex or very simple – depending on whether there are already experiences, ideas and procedures that can be applied to the case at hand.

If one asks the question whether elves exist or not, one comes one step further, if one asks oneself first of all, by what one would recognize an elf as real. The most important characteristic a flower spirit would have to have in order to be called such would be a consciousness and an individuality.

How can this be proven? One can, of course, make dream journeys to various plants and will find that one can talk to them – but is that a sure proof that there is a plant consciousness? It is first of all only the proof that one can receive information about plants with the help of dream journeys and then experience these internally as pictures and conversations – and possibly also that this information can be very helpful.

III 3.   Plant telepathy

So one has to go back one step further with the question: How would I know that a plant has a consciousness?

This question is not easy to answer – but since I have already done experiments on it, I know fortunately which approach has been successful in the end. Asking a good question is generally already half the answer …

The first interesting observation was my mother's "green thumb" – she was able to make all plants bloom again that others had already given up on.

When I was once told about the experiment where you take two identical plants and curse one and praise and encourage the other, whereupon the first reacts by wilting and the second by thriving, I found this completely plausible based on my experience with my mother's "green thumb". When I also did the experiment myself once, the results matched what I had been told.

Interestingly, my mother once told me that she sometimes threatened plants that did not want to thrive with throwing them on the compost – whereupon they always started to grow.

What does it mean that plants react in this way? After all, they do not have ears and do not speak the human language. So information from a human being arrives at a plant – the plants apparently perceive what the human being imagines.

Even if one argues that it is not the words of the human being, but the changes in the life force of the plants caused by the words, it still remains that the plants can perceive the feelings and words and pictures of a human being "telepathically". Thus, the plant has the ability to perceive and react to non-physical things, i.e. the plants have telepathic perception.

The ability of perception is not identical with a consciousness, but perceptions are what a part of the contents of a consciousness consists of – and without perceptions, thus without contents of consciousness, a consciousness would be quite functionless and therefore also useless.

There is another experiment with which one can prove the plant telepathy:

Cleve Backster, an employee of the American secret service, connected a lie detector to his dragon tree in 1966 in order to measure how long it takes water to get from the roots to the top of the plant. However, instead of a rash indicating rising humidity in the plant, he found the rash that occurs in people who have been asked an unpleasant question.

Backster then tried all sorts of things, which the plant found boring and therefore did not respond. When he had the thought of burning one of its leaves, however, the polygraph struck out – the dragon tree had apparently sensed Backster's thoughts.

The dragon tree even seemed to sympathize with other plants, as the polygraph connected to it even struck out when Backster hurt other plants near the dragon tree. So it would appear that the plants that are in the same location are telepathically connected to each other. This suggests that also in nature the meadows, plant beds, groups of trees, forests etc. are not only an "optical unit" but also a "telepathic network".

III 4. Plant-memory

About 15 years ago, together with my friend Jörg, I made a dream journey into a homeopathic globule of club moss (Lycopodium), because Jörg wanted to get to know this remedy better.

The pictures of this dream journey started on a rather bare gravel beach, where we were picked up by a huge white bird, which told us that it should take us to the King of the Forests. So we got on the bird and flew over the sea.

After a while, however, the bird got a stiff left shoulder, so that we all threatened to fall into the sea. Then I put my hand on the shoulder joint and sent life force into the joint, whereupon the giant bird could fly on normally again.

Finally we came to a new shore, which also seemed quite barren. Jörg and I took two different paths and both found a slightly swampy valley full of trees unknown to us, where we met again.

When we asked where the King of the Forests was, we found a small pavilion on a hill – but there was no one there. When we searched inwardly for the king, we sensed that he was deep down in the earth.

So I dived down a good 100m into the earth. That was quite uncomfortable because I felt like I was diving through a huge mass grave. Far down at the bottom of this mass grave I then found the King of the Forests lying there – and I have never before seen such a resigned and depressed being as this king.

I took him to the surface in the pavilion, where Jörg and I placed him in the sun-light, thinking that this would brighten him up a bit – but the effect was quite small.

After we returned from the dream trip, Jörg told me that Lycopodium is given to people who have resigned themselves, who believe that their great time is already over and who are merely hanging on and have at least retained a sense of justice – a typical Lycopodium patient is, for example, the aging, lonely notary with a stiff left shoulder like the giant bird.

When we researched what is known about Lycopodium on the Internet, we found that during the Carboniferous period, 360-300 million years ago, the earth was covered primarily by Lycopodium – at that time, Lycopodium was truly the King of the Forests.

From the huge Lycopodium forests of that time, only the small Lycopodium weed at the edge of the forest is left – the great time of Lycopodium is over …

From the Lycopodium trees of that time, all the hard coal, lignite, petroleum and natural gas have been created … a huge Lycopodium mass grave …

Thus, the effect of the homeopathic remedy prepared from Lycopodium and administered to "resigned notaries with stiff left shoulder" does not correspond to the ingredients of the plant from which this remedy is prepared, but to the history of this plant. This means that Lycopodium as a plant genus has a memory that goes back far beyond the individual plant to the time 360 million years ago.

The same observation, i.e. the dependence of its effect on its history rather than on its constituents, can also be made with other homeopathic remedies – but it is particularly impressive with Lycopodium.

III 5.   Plant-consciousness

Thus, there are now already two elements that can be said about plant spirits: they have telepathic perception and they have plant memory. If now the ability of perception is combined with the ability of memory, the result is the ability to recognize a current perception as something known.

This process obviously takes place in the consciousness – which would prove that plants have a consciousness.

The memory of these elves encompasses the memories of 360 million years – this memory must therefore be a part of the collective (sub-)consiousness of these elves.

III 6.   Help from the Lycopodium Elf

Some years later I once visited an acquaintance who wanted to buy a house, but the whole family found that the house in question had a rather unpleasant appearance. After taking a thorough look at the house, we found that the huge oil tank in the basement, which held enough heating oil for several years, was the cause of this unpleasant aura.

Thereupon I got Lycopodium C200 as drops and went down to the boiler room with my friend's wife and asked the woman to simply sing notes for the King of the Woods (she is a pianist). While doing this, I went around the tank and sprinkled the Lycopodium C200 on the tank, inwardly calling the King of Woods and asking him to dissolve the emanation of this oil tank.

The Lycopodium elf was very cooperative and granted our request, so that the house felt much better afterwards.

III 7.   Help from the Laurel Elf

Again a few years later I was with a friend on the Canary Island of La Palma. On my birthday we hiked through the valley where the last laurel forest on earth is located. Since my friend could not run well uphill, she was exhausted quite soon and has sat down on a rock at the wayside – at the place we have been about 30m above the valley bottom.

As I stood there looking down into the valley and thinking that these laurel forests had once been very widespread, I had the idea of calling the laurel forest elf. I had hardly had this thought when I saw him too – he was standing down in the valley and was so huge that we were at eye level. He didn't seem like a lovely flower spirit either, but was 35m tall, stocky and robust and a bit restrained, though at the same time, well, I can best describe it as "life friendly".

I greeted him and asked him if he could give my friend some strength to keep walking. He nodded, glanced briefly at her, and then continued up the valley.

My perception was like a dream journey with open eyes, where the inner and outer images overlay each other.

My friend clearly felt the "blessing" of the laurel elf (she did not know that I had just seen him) and actually felt fit again, and instead of turning back we were able to continue walking up the valley for another half hour.

III 8.   A gift of the meadowfoam

Some of my encounters with plant elves have also been simply beautiful …

When I was about 23 years old, while walking in the woods, I found a meadow that was full of meadowfoam. For some reason, I was very touched by this sight and I knelt down in front of one of these flowers, held my hand next to it and told it how beautiful I thought it was.

Then I suddenly got visions of flowers – the images glowed from within and the flowers had the richest colors and the most varied shapes and kept changing into more and more beautiful images.

For about a year, all I had to do was think of that meadowfoam in the forest meadow to conjure up those flower visions again – that has been a really great gift from the meadowfoam elves.

III 9.   The collective subconsciousness of plants

After the proof that there are indeed plant elves as a "collective plant consciousness", we can now take a closer look at whether we can find out more about this plant consciousness and thus about the elves.

There is a well known phenomenon in homeopathy, which is interesting in this context: The effect of a homeopathic remedy does not begin with the taking of the remedy, but with the decision of the homeopath, which remedy he wants to give. The trigger of the effect is apparently the telepathic connection established by the homeopath's decision between the remedy and the patient (who is willing to take the remedy). Also in this case the homeopathic remedy, in the case of Lycopodium thus the plant-elf, reacts to a telepathic information.

Due to this dynamic, instead of taking the remedy itself, it is also possible to write the name of the remedy and its dosage (e.g. "Lycopodium C200, three globules") on a piece of paper, pour water over this piece of paper, collect the water in a glass and then drink the water.

Taking the globules or drops is a symbolic-magical gesture that seals a connection with the plant elf – a magical contract, so to speak.

This ancient method has also been used in Egypt against snakebites: People poured water over a statue of the goddess Isis, who healed her son Horus from a snake bite, and then drank this water. This method is recommended in homeopathy when there is no possibility to get the needed remedy.

13

III 10. Elves, dwarfs and animal spirits

In homeopathy there are mainly three types of remedies: Remedies made from animals, from plants, and from minerals.

One can tell from a patient's behavior which of these three groups the remedy he needs comes from:

> If the patient is all about an action, he needs an animal remedy: animals have a dynamic of movement.

> If the patient is all about posture, he needs a herbal remedy: plants have posture first and foremost.

> If the patient is all about a structure, he needs a mineral remedy: minerals have mainly a structure (crystallization type).

In general, animals will have consciousness, and for plants consciousness can also be proven by the observations just described.

Since the mineral remedies in homoeopathy do not behave differently from the animal and vegetable remedies, one should be able to assume that the minerals also have a consciousness – their effect depends also on their history.

III 11. What is consciousness?

One may ask what consciousness actually is. Is it something which exists only selectively and which must first be generated? Or is consciousness simply the inside of what appears on its outside as matter?

This second description fits at least better to the different magic phenomena which can be explained more easily with this model. If one understands the consciousness as the inside of all things and this inside is just as much a continuum as the material "outside of the world", then one can influence his environment from his body as well as from his consciousness. The second case describes most magical phenomena: consciousness acts on matter.

This second model would also facilitate the description of the considerations about the elves: If everything also has a consciousness, then also everything can telepathically, i.e. on the level of consciousness, get in contact with each other, exchange information and have an effect – just perform magic …

III 12.   The Three Allies

The three homeopathic categories of animal, vegetable and mineral remedies are found in a place that plays a greater role in magic.

If one frequently performs dream journeys, vision quests, meditations and the like, there is a high probability that sooner or later one will meet one's own power animal. This power animal embodies one's own dynamics, one's own way of acting, one's own instincts, one's own way of moving, partly also the form of sensory perceptions, needs, sexual inclinations, social habits and the like.

Besides the power animal, you can also find a power plant that represents your own attitude: the way you stand in life, the way you hold your body, and also the place you prefer to be in the world.

Finally, there is the power stone, which vividly embodies one's structure: how one thinks, how one orders one's world, what forms one builds, and the like.

When a soul incarnates, it takes its place in a fertilized ovum. Through the orgasm of the two parents at conception, life force is released, which gathers around the fertilized egg, from which the life force body of the embryo with the seven chakras is formed.

This rotating ball of life force is shaped on the one hand by the body of the embryo and on the other hand also by the character of the soul and its intention for this life. Since in the area of life force there is the principle "same and same are happy together", the animal is attached to this sphere of life force shaped by the soul, which corresponds best to the character and intention of the soul in terms of its dynamics, furthermore the plant, whose attitude corresponds best to the character and intention of the soul, and finally still the mineral, whose structure corresponds best to the character and intention of the soul.

By the power animal is meant, of course, no real, physical animal, but so to speak the spirit of this kind of animal. The same applies to the power plant and the power stone: the connection arises to the respective plant elf and to the stone "dwarf", if one wants to call the stone spirit in such a way.

Consequently, every human being has an elf as a friend and ally throughout his life – and additionally also an animal spirit and a stone dwarf.

These three spirits form together with the soul the basic features of the own individual mythology. This can probably be illustrated most simply by an example:

> The soul of a human being is a drop from the "sea of a deity". A soul can be, for example, a small part of Osiris. Such a soul will seek constant, cyclical transformation because Osiris is the grain god. It will also focus its gaze on self-discovery because Osiris is also the god of the dead and thus the god of

the soul. The afterlife journey is also an essential part of this person's mythology, since Osiris dies at every harvest and then is reborn in springtime. Such a person could be a shaman, a therapist, an explorer of the psyche, an astrologer, and the like.

A suitable power animal for such a person would be a wolf, since the wolf is the afterlife guide in the myths.

A suitable power plant could be the thuja, which in the myths is the connection between this world and the hereafter – e.g. as the cabbalistic Tree of Life.

A matching power stone could be the rock crystal, since its main property is clarity and integrating (a rock crystal ist transparent and consists of only one molecule).

There are many connections between these four beings, both in the myths and in the homeopathic remedies (Lac Lupi for the wolf, Thula occidentalis for the Thuja and Silicea for the rock crystal). So the choice and combination of the three allies of a soul is not arbitrary: The three allies form an organic group – even from the homeopathic point of view.

The combination of Thuja, which is also called "Tree of Life", with the rock crystal, for example, suggests an inclination to the Kabbalistic Tree of Life – especially since the homeopathic remedy Thula occidentalis is associated with esoteric inclinations. Furthermore, a wolf appears now and then in the dreams and dream journeys to Thuja.

III 13.   The Sushumna and the Tree of Life

One can take the consideration of the elves even further: What in man is generally a correspondence to the plants?

It should be something upright, something that has a posture – that is the sushumna, the central, vertical life force channel where the seven chakras are located, which can be understood as the flowers on this trunk. The two side channels, Ida and Pingala, would then be two branches of this tree.

The Kabbalistic Tree of Life also has a trunk ("Middle Pillar"), two branches on the side ("Left Pillar" and "Right Pillar") and eleven flowers ("Sephiroth").

Both the chakra tree and the Kabbalistic Tree of Life have a tall, slender shape – just as a thuja looks like.

III 14.   The World Tree

The original plant in the myths is the world tree, which connects this world on earth (trunk), the underworld under the earth (roots) and the heaven beyond (crown).

Against this background, the dance of the elves under the world tree then again becomes an image which is more than just a romantic fantasy …

III 15.   Forms of Consciousness

At this point, one can, if one wishes, still think one step further.

For this, first of all the general proof of telepathy is necessary – which fortunately is quite easily possible:

> For this experiment one needs at least five persons, preferably a larger group of people like a class in school. One person gets two dozen postcards, photos and the like with striking motifs and puts them into envelopes and seals them so that the pictures cannot be seen.
>
> Then four people each receive an envelope, which they place between them on the table. Then everyone concentrates for about 3 minutes on the postcard in the envelope and then writes down their perceptions.
>
> Afterwards, the perceptions that occur in at least three persons are combined – e.g. sand, warmth, predominantly blue, a bright or yellow spot in the upper right corner. This possibly results in a beach scene with the sun in the upper right corner.
>
> This image is then supplemented by the motifs that appeared in at least two people – e.g. a palm tree and something angular white in the center of the image in the blue. So it seems to be the picture of a palm tree beach with the sun and a ship with a white sail.
>
> Then each group opens their envelope and looks at the postcard that they previously described telepathically.
>
> This simple method makes it possible to distinguish the telepathic perceptions (which coincide in several people) from the associations (which occur only in one person).

Telepathy is not a "private affair", but something that can coordinate the consciousnesses of two or more people. This can be experienced most impressively on group dream journeys, on which it happens again and again that one sees something, which the other also sees and then speaks out.

> I once made a dream journey to the dragons with a woman, during which we rode on a dragon. Suddenly the dragon had to stop because it had injured its right front paw. When I said that out loud, the woman had to laugh because she had just dismounted in her dream journey to examine the dragon's right front foot.
> Such things happen on almost every group dream journey – one is indeed traveling in the same image.

If one now takes all the things considered here together – i.e. the proof of telepathy, the consciousness of plants, the telepathy of plants, the telepathic coordination during group dream journeys, the telepathic contact with objects – then it follows that all things are or can be telepathically connected with each other. Further, it follows from homeopathy that all things – humans, animals, plants, minerals – have a memory. Consequently, all things have consciousness.

Furthermore, all these consciousnesses are telepathically coupled or at least have the possibility to be.

This "telepathic connection between the consciousnesses in all things" is, so to speak, a general collective subconsciousness, which does not only include human beings. The collective subconsciousness of a plant species would then be the elf of this plant species.

The telepathic connection of the collective subconsciousness of humans, all animal species, all plant species and all mineral species then already comes very close to the consciousness of the earth often called "Gaia".

IV   Elf Encounters

Since, in the end, the things that are of importance are those that are enriching, the question also arises in the consideration of the elves, what one can experience with them – and how people have used this in the past and today.

IV 1.   Vitality

There is a great benefit of contact with the elves, but it is not easy to put into words. Probably most people will know the effect of a walk through the forest, across the heath, or through a herb meadow in the mountains. Are there elves involved in this? Or is it a purely physical effect on humans through more oxygen, through the spicier scent of the air, through the quieter environment?

At least also the sight of the plants has an effect on humans – not only the increased O_2 content of the air.

You can look at a group of trees consciously and play with your own perception: You can look at the trees with your mind and estimate how much they might be worth as lumber. You can also look at them with fear, fearing that a rabid fox is about to come out from behind them. There is the possibility to look "at" the trees, i.e. objectively and soberly only at their surface.

A somewhat more creative possibility is to look "into" the trees. This does not mean an "X-ray view", but rather a "groping for the life force". If this is successful, if you can make contact with the trees in this way, everything feels much more alive and you get into a "child's wonder" about everything you see.

This way of looking is similar to trying to look at everything you see as if you were seeing it for the first time.

This way of looking can also occur spontaneously. I experienced it for the first time while walking in the forest, when a blade of grass on the side of the path suddenly seemed to glow from within. I crouched down in front of the blade of grass and looked at it for several minutes, completely moved. This was not a visual, external glow, but an "inner glow" – as if I were perceiving its life force.

That was a very fulfilling experience!

You can also try to feel the aura of a tree. To do this, you either place your hands on the bark of the tree or hold your hands a short distance in front of the tree. This is similar to sensing a person's life force in mesmerism, reiki, or other methods of using the life force.

19

While in humans this life force feels like an electric-tingling heat, the life force of trees makes more of an airy-flowing and "thinner" impression. Trees differ very clearly in the quality of their life force: the lark feels warm-airy, the acacia hard-airy, the pine fiery-airy, the beech cool-watery, the oak warm-earthy, the yew warm-earthy-sterling, and so on.

If one has generally realized that there are elves, one can consider this touching of the life force of the trees as a first contact in which one can get to know the general temperament of a tree species – one reaches out to the tree elf, so to speak.

You can also try to visually perceive the life force of a tree. In my experience so far, this is easiest when the sun is just above the horizon in the morning or evening and shines on the bark of the trees.

But since everyone is different, it's best to playfully see which way you perceive something – perhaps dusk or the light of the full moon is also most appropriate for some people, or a prolonged previous fast …

Sometimes, through the occupation with the plant elves, one also finds unexpected memories of plants that one knew in childhood: the cherry tree in the garden, the red thorn in front of the front door, the old oak tree in the kindergarten, the dandelion on the meadow of the grandparents …

These memories, of course, do not say anything about the existence of elves and they are in no way something objective, but they open again the level in the person where one simply perceives what is there. This form of "non-intellectual perception" is already very close to the perception of the life force of plants – and the elves are the life force of plants.

This "wondering perception" is completely independent of whether it leads on to a perception of the life force, a great enrichment of everyday life – the world seems much more alive again through this form of childlike looking.

I was once in northern Spain about thirty years ago at a Rainbow Camp. One day I climbed up into the mountains and found a circle of about a dozen beech trees in a meadow. They were so close together that you could just walk between them into the middle of them.

There in the middle of them it felt like I was standing in the beech trees instead of between them – that's how much they shaped the space within their circle with their own quality.

There is a small birch grove near here in the Kottenforst that I often pass when I am in the forest. For some reason not quite clear to me, I have never entered this patch of forest, although I have otherwise looked at every corner of the Kottenforst. Only the meeting place of the wild pigs at a remote marshy corner in the Kottenforst I have never entered – for the sake of the wild pigs.

With this birch grove I always had the feeling that a spirit lives there, which does not want to be disturbed, which I also respected gladly – similarly as I would not sit down in a church also on the altar.

In the course of time, three women with whom I have passed by this birch grove on various occasions have told me independently of each other that they see or sense a faun there every time. This is not a general "Kottenforst myth", since these women had never heard of it before, nor had they told anyone else about it themselves – they knew that I would understand what the said.

What kind of "spirit" lives in this birch grove? Is it a faun or the birch elf? Or does the birch elf take the form of a faun? Unfortunately, I have not yet seen this birch forest spirit myself visually – neither internally (dream journey) nor externally (with the eyes).

Also some other people, with whom I have passed this birch grove, found that this grove is very powerful.

IV 2. Power plants

One's power plant can help one understand one's attitude in life – both one's body posture and one's inner attitude toward the things one experiences. Often the stories one can find in legends and fairy tales about the plant in question also fit one's own life very well.

The descriptions found in homeopathy about the plant in question often clearly show some of one's own character traits. In some cases, cross connections to one's own power animal or power stone also appear, which gives the impression that certain combinations of power animal, power plant and power stone are particularly common – as if there were firm friendships between them.

I have come to know over 50 different power animals through the dream journeys I conduct with people, but since I did not also pay attention to the power plants in the beginning, I do not know enough combinations of these three allies to be able to say whether there are a lot of preferred combinations of these three allies.

There is a distinct difference between the power animals, the power plants, and the power stones: The power animals have a consciousness like a normal, physically existing animal, but the power plants and the power stones have only a collective consciousness. This collective consciousness in the case of the plants and stones corresponds in the case of the animals to the mother goddess of the animal species in question: the White Wolf or Moon-Wolf, the White Elephant, the White Buffalo Woman (Pte-san-win), the Great Orca, the Stag with the sun in his antlers, the Egyptian animal-gods, and so on.

IV 3.   Homeopathy and Bach Flowers

The many herbal remedies of homeopathy are a very practical approach to the plants from which they are made. By taking these remedies, one can on the one hand cure diseases, but on the other hand also get to know these plants.

The same is true for the Bach flowers, which are also herbal remedies that use the life force of the plants and not their physical substance.

IV 4.   Healing through Elves

My son David had problems with the miniscus in both knees at the end of his school years and was due for surgery. On his graduation trip, which took place shortly before the scheduled surgery, he went to the castle in Nuremberg. When he was standing up there with his two crutches, he remembered a method I had once shown him.

It involves telling your body what you want and then waiting to see what it does. This method is similar to commuting and automatic writing, except that you move your entire body – without consciously controlling it yourself, of course.

So David told his body to heal itself. David then "automatically" went to a door in the castle courtyard, which he had not noticed before. It opened and he found himself in a herb garden on top of the battlements of the castle wall. He walked purposefully in this "automatic way" to one of the last beds in this garden, tilted his upper body forward, grabbed an herb and (still automatically) put it in his mouth and swallowed it. This all happened in one fluid motion and completely by surprise for David – as is typical for these automatic sequences of movements.

Then he tried walking without crutches – and had no more pain. Then he put the crutches under his arm and went back to the others in his class and didn't need any more surgery and is now a top athlete (Parcour and Ninja Warrior).

IV 5.   Conversations with trees

You can have a conversation with trees and with other plants. This is easiest if you already have some experience with dream journeys, family constellations, automatic writing and similar methods that promote contact into the subconscious from which telepathy emanates.

What one can learn from trees and in what things they are wise, one will only be able to find out through one's own conversations with trees.

One should take everything one hears seriously, but not simply believe it. It makes sense to check what you hear as well as possible, possibly apply it carefully, look at the results, and then possibly seek a new conversation with the tree.

This is not much different from a conversation with a person you do not know yet. However, there is also the fact that you may have to understand the plant's point of view and the images it uses, which also is not so different from meeting a new person.

IV 6.   Magic rings

When around 1985 the forest was suffering a lot from acid rain, I became a member of Robin Wood, the forest section of Greenpeace. At that time I thought that it should be possible to do something against the dying of the forest with the help of magic.

It seemed to me that strengthening the forest by burying magic rings in the forest would be the most appropriate way. When I talked to various trees about this, I was told again and again that the problem was not a lack of vitality in the forest, which I wanted to remedy with the rings, but the acid rain – and that this must be changed by people.

However, I did not want to hear that and made the magic rings nevertheless – which logically became a complete failure.

IV 7.   Crop circles

The crop circles appear since approx. 1920 – as the name already says – predominantly in crop fields. Only since approx. 1995 they appear quite sporadically also in rape fields and the like. So it is obvious that these crop circles have something to do with the grain.

In the beginning, these crop circles were just simple circular areas of flattened grain; in the meantime, however, they have developed into very complicated patterns, which represent, among other things, the mathematically very complex "Mandelbrot set", the equally complex "Julia set" or parts of the cabbalistic tree of life.

When you stand in a crop circle that has just been created, you feel an intense energy – the typical electric-tingling heat that you can also feel in the life force of a human being. However, it is much stronger and at the same time "calmer". The different parts of a fresh crop circle also feel distinctly different.

This crop circle phenomenon can be understood most likely as a form of telekinesis – only from whom does this telekinesis proceed? From the grain, that is, from the grain elf? From the grain god? From the humans? From the earth?

The many motives from mathematics, mythology and the like, which are found in the crop circles, make it probable that these crop circles at least in recent time do not originate independently from the inner pictures of the people, thus independently from the collective subconsciousness of the people.

Since otherwise no collective telekinesis of the people is known, whose strength is known to the purposeful bending of grain stalks on an area of the size of a soccer field, one can assume that not only the collective subconsciousness of the people, but probably also the earth itself is involved in this phenomenon. A conversation of the earth with the people with participation of the grain elf?

However, these are all at best "educated guesses" and not sure explanations. However, a participation of the elves of the different grain types seems to be quite probable – however this participation may look concretely.

V   Plant-Gods

The term "elf-gods" sounds unfamiliar, even if it can be understood without much effort – the term "plant-gods" sounds more familiar, even if it is also unusual. However, if you take a closer look at the different mythologies, you will find quite a number of beings that can most likely be called "plant gods" or "elf gods".

The fact that an elf has become a deity, or that a deity has been closely associated with a plant, is of course not further proof that elves actually exist, but it does show that some plants have been so important to humans that they have become deities.

These plant deities should ultimately be the same kind of beings as the plant elves.

V 1.   Hathor

The Egyptian mother goddess Hathor was represented in various guises: as a woman, as a cow, as a sky, and as a tree. This tree was the world tree, which was the way from the earth to the heaven-beyond, which Hathor embodied as mother-goddess and cow.

In this Hathor-motif the way to the goddess was identified with the goddess herself, so that she could be represented as a tree with a woman's head, breasts and human arms.

Hathor is therefore very probably not a former tree elf, but a goddess who has been associated with a tree symbol (the world tree as the path to the afterlife).

V 2.   Inanna

With the goddess Inanna, who is the Sumerian equivalent to the Egyptian Hathor, it looks similar: She is the mother goddess who has been associated with the world tree, from whose wood the god Dumuzi made her bed and her throne for her.

Inanna is thus also a tree-goddess, but not a tree-elf.

V 3. Osiris

The Egyptian god Osiris is the embodiment of grain. Germination is the birth of Osiris and harvest is his death. Osiris is consequently a grain elf.

However, the germination of grain and the harvest of grain have also been equated to the birth and death of humans, which is why Osiris has also been the god of the dead and the god of rebirth in the otherworld of the Egyptians.

The question arises whether Osiris was first an ancestor, who was then associated with agriculture, or whether he was first an embodiment of grain and only afterwards also became the god of the dead. Since the ancestor is the older motif, Osiris will probably have emerged from the ancestor. Osiris, however, has been so closely associated with grain that he may be taken to be the grain elf of the Egyptians.

There was an Osiris ceremony which very clearly represents the conception of Osiris as the grain: In the spring, the Egyptians made small statuettes from a mixture of earth and a little grain in the shape of the reclining, dead Osiris – that is, Osiris as a mummy. This statuette was then kept moist for several days, causing the grain in the statuette to begin to sprout: Osiris was reborn!

If you want to get to know elves better, it is worthwhile to perform this simple ceremony yourself.

Osiris was also a tree god in two ways:

First, his coffin grew into a tree and then drifted across the sea to a distant land where the coffin was found by Isis, who is the sister, wife, rebirth lover, rebirth mother and rebirth nurse of Osiris. Here the sea is the water underworld and the tree is the world tree – both lead to the afterlife goddess Isis.

On the other hand, the backbone of Osiris is conceived as a tree called "Djed", meaning "constancy". Here the backbone has been associated with the world tree because of its resemblance to a tree.

Osiris has consequently been associated with the world tree in the same way as the goddess Hathor. Osiris is thus a tree-god, but not a tree-elf – he is, however, the grain-elf.

V 4. Idun

The Germanic goddess Idun is the goddess of the apple tree, on which grow the apples that give immortality to the gods. This motif obviously goes back to the rebirth ideas, which is why the apple tree will be the world tree.

In this function it appears also with the Celts (with whom the beyond island is called "Avalon"; i.e. "apple island"), with the Greeks (the golden apples of the Hesperides) and still some other peoples.

The apples from this tree have later often been reinterpreted as death apples: the death apple of Merlin's ex-wife among the Celts, the death apple of the Slavs, Eve's apple in the Bible, the deadly apple of Snow White's stepmother, and so on.

Idun, then, like Hathor, is not a tree elf, but a goddess associated with the world tree. Of course, this does not exclude at all that one can learn something about the apples on dream journeys to Idun …

V 5. Soma, Haoma, Kwasir and Medigenus

The Indo-Europeans brewed and drank in ritual a potion that was supposed to give them immortality in the afterlife, profound knowledge in this world and an elevated, serene state of consciousness. This potion consisted of water, honey, milk and a plant extract, among other things. The milk was originally the milk of the goddess of the afterlife when nursing the reborn dead again after rebirth in the afterlife. This milk then took on the symbolism of rebirth.

The Indians named this potion as "Soma" after the plant whose extract they used for this potion. The potion and the plant are explicitly regarded as a deity – the Soma elf has thus been elevated to a god.

Among the Persians, who are closely related to the Indians, this plant, this potion and this god were called "Haoma".

The Teutons called this potion "Kwasir". He also appears personified in the myths as a wise man, created together by the gods. With the Teutons, however, it is no longer recognizable that this potion also contained a plant extract – even though they certainly made herbal beer.

With the Celts this god was called "Medigenus" – "the mead-born one". This god of the mead has a relation to the honey, from which the mead was brewed, but no more to a certain plant.

V 6. Dagda

The Celtic father of the gods, Dagda, has been closely associated with hazel bushes, which have had the same symbolism as apple trees among the Celts and Germanic peoples. This symbolism comes from the builders of the megalithic sites in Spain, Portugal and France, where the hazelnut originated.

Again, the god has only been associated with the world tree, but he is not himself a plant elf.

The Germanic apple goddess Idun and the Germanic earth goddess Jörd have also been associated with the hazelnut bush.

V 7. Hun Nah Yeh

The god "Hun Nah Yeh" is the Mayan corn god. He dies at sowing and he is reborn at sprouting – this is the same symbolism as Osiris. Hun Nah Yeh is consequently the corn elf.

Humans ate the corn and they were once created from the corn in Mayan myths. Hun Nah Yeh is therefore like Osiris also a god of the dead and the archetype of humans and their ancestor. Just as the pharaoh in Egypt saw himself as Osiris or as a descendant of Osiris, the king of the Mayas saw himself as an embodiment of Hun Nah Yeh.

These myths arise from the equation of the sowing, germination and the death of the corn with the procreation, birth and death of man.

The corn god, as the "first man" in time, was of course also the god of the king, who had been the "first man" in rank.

V 8. Cinteotl

The corn god Cinteotl is the Toltec-Aztec equivalent of the Mayan corn god Hun Nah Yeh.

Cinteotl is like Hun Nah Yeh and like Osiris the corn elf.

V 9. Yum Kaax

The Mayan god "Yum Kaax" is the embodiment of vegetation and forest and wild animals. He was invoked by hunters for help before hunting. So Yum Kaax is a wilderness god – comparable to Seth of the Egyptians.

It is thus quite certain that Yum Kaax embodies above all the antithesis of the corn god and the cultivated land, and is not a "general plant elf."

V 10. Xochiquetzal

The Aztec goddess Xochiquetzal is the goddess of flowers, but also the goddess of the moon, earth, love, dances and games. She thus seems to correspond to Venus of the Romans and Aphrodite of the Greeks – a goddess of love and beauty, and originally probably the re-creation mistress of the dead in the afterlife.

However, since her name means "flower-feather," flowers seem to play a greater role for her. At her feast, dancers appeared in animal and plant costumes.

However, it seems to be very daring to think of her as an elf-goddess – her connections to plants are too vague for that …

V 11. Chicomecoatl

The name of this Aztec goddess means "Seven Serpents". This name indicates that she was a goddess of the earth and probably also of the underworld, since the snakes are the ancestral spirits. She was also considered a goddess of food and especially a goddess of corn. However, her connection to the corn probably arose secondarily from her function as earth goddess – the corn grows on the earth.

So she will not be a corn elf.

V 12. Xilonen

She is also a corn goddess – her name means "the hairy one" and refers to the threads on the cob of corn. Xilonen was primarily responsible for the young corn.

However, given the general Central American symbolism, she is more likely to be an earth goddess who gives the corn to the people, rather than an embodiment of the corn itself – that is, not "Mrs. Corn," but the "Corn Mother."

Several people were sacrificed to this Aztec goddess on June 24 (midsummer), and some time later another girl. The sacrificial blood was poured over the statue of the goddess to give her strength.

V 13. Sara Mama

The name of the goddess "Sara Mama" means "Corn Mother." This goddess of the Quetchua Indians of Peru (who are often mistakenly called "Incas") corresponds to the Aztec goddess Xilonen – she is not the corn itself, but the mother of corn and the corn god. She also corresponds to the Egyptian Isis, who is the mother of the corn god Osiris.

V 14. Ilmatecutli

This Aztec goddess was responsible for the ripe corn. Probably, like Xilonen, she was originally an earth goddess.

V 15. Xochipilli

This Aztec god, whose name means "prince of flowers," is a god of procreative power, music, dance, and corn. He was also called "Macuilxochitl," meaning "Five Flowers." He is often represented together with plant tendrils, among which there are some hallucinogenic plants that played a role in the cult of the Aztecs.

Xochipilli thus seems to be a combination of "reborn god" (procreative power), corn god (who is also reborn), and ritual potion god (a correspondence to the Soma god of the Indians and the Haoma god of the Persians).

So Xochipilli could be a plant-elf in several ways: as a corn-elf and as the elf of several drug-plants.

V 15. Oberon

The elf king Oberon does not appear in Western Europe until the 13th century. He is probably one of the many variants of the Germanic Alberich ("elf-king"), who is a figure of the former father of the gods, Tyr, in the afterlife as king of the dead. In connection with these ideas, the elves are still the ancestral spirits of the Germanic tribes, who have been called "Alfen" or "Alben".

Oberon is best known through Shakespeare's "Midsummer Night's Dream".

V 16. Totem poles

Totem poles have existed since the late Paleolithic period — probably for about 50,000 years. They are found on every continent except Africa. They depict a human being and his soul bird. Already in the early Neolithic period, 12,000 years ago, there were several stone totem poles in Göbekli Tepe in northern Mesopotamia and in the wider area around this temple-mountain, depicting panther men with two Kundalini serpents, two-headed goddesses with soul birds, and the like. This symbolism is found almost unchanged even 7000 years later in the early cultures of Sumer and Egypt.

These forerunners of the Egyptian Hathor as a tree goddess and of Osiris as a tree god will not be plant elves, but "deities of the world tree", although it cannot be excluded that the people in the late Paleolithic and in the early Neolithic still understood the trees, from which they created their totem poles, as living beings.

Therefore, there might have been an association between the totem poles and the tree spirits (elves) – but this is only a very vague assumption.

VI Dream journeys to the elves

In the following, three examples of dream journeys to plants are given in order to make more vivid the nature of the conversations with the plants, their very different character and their "mythological background".

The three plants chosen here as examples are chamomile, peppermint and sage.

I carried out these dream journeys together with a friend.

When in the following dream journeys the plants speak, I have spoken out what I have heard the plant speak inwardly.

During these dream journeys we speak out and record (on computer) everything that we see and hear on the dream journeys. Immediately afterwards, I listen to the recording and type it all out while my memory is still fresh.

More of these dream-journeys may be found in my book „Traumreisen zu Heilpflanzen".

VI 1. Chamomile

Harry: "Hello Chamomile, we would like to meet you. Would you like to tell us something about yourself?" ...

Chamomile: "Yes." ... ...

Harry: "I have a feeling you don't want to say anything, but show pictures and smells?"

Chamomile: "Yes."

Harry: "Well, I'm going to smell – let's see ... ... I feel like I smell chamomile, or at least something that smells like it ... there's something calm, sustaining ... it's enveloping ... there's something very archaic about it ... like breast milk is something very archaic ... I don't know what it reminds me of ... hm, oddly enough, it reminds me of the scabs that newborn babies have on their heads. "

Jule: "Hm ..."

Harry: "It's curious ... ... Chamomile asks me what it is that happens inside me when I smell it. ... ... It has something of a feeling of security, although I've noticed that I first have to get involved somehow ..."

Jule: "I already smelled it on the way here (inside)." (We had arranged to travel to the chamomile today.)

Harry: "Oh ..."
Jule: "On the bike ..."
Harry (laughing): "Hm ..."
Jule: "It's quite warm, too, the smell."
Harry: "Yes." ...
Jule: "And there's something earthy about it, I think, so ... so powerful ..."
Harry: "Hm ... yes, that's right – with 'security' I usually don't think of something powerful ... but this scent has both." ... ...
Harry: "Chamomile – is there anything in particular you want me to do?"
Chamomile: "Wait."
Harry: "Yes, fine." ... ...
Harry: "I feel like this chamomile scent or quality is enveloping me." ... ...
Harry: "So almost like being in my mother's womb, actually ... ... the chamomile smiles." ... ...
Harry: "What's going on with you right now, Jule?"
Jule: "I just remembered that I was given chamomile, chamomile essential oil, ehm, as a gift when Daisy (her daughter) was born." ...
Harry: "Hm ..."
Jule: "And that ... that was quite blue ... and that also has something ... something powerful ... but at the same time also something cool – so I said 'warming' earlier and it is also warm, but somehow also cool ... I can't really ... really explain what I mean ..."
Harry: "Is it something like sobering up, clearing up, bringing down to earth?"
Jule: "Nah ... ... maybe something balancing, that you're neither too hot nor too cold ... uh, I don't know ... I don't know if that's right." ... ...
Harry (laughs): "I keep seeing the chamomile as a child's face ... that has just tilted its head a little to the left and is smirking a little bit and looks like 'Well, what's next? Is she hitting it now? She's slowly getting closer'."
Jule (laughs): "I have a Kamilla in kindergarten ... that's one of my heart kids." ...
Harry: "When you said that, 'Don Camillo and Peppone' came to mind."
We both laugh ...
Jule: "And Kamilla in kindergarten, she's got an Italian father and ... a mother from Brazil, and she's so fiery, it's unbelievable! And at the same time she's like 'I want to sit on your lap' and she's really, really, really tender ... and that's such a beautiful mixture!" ... ...
Harry: "I asked Chamomile if she could show me ... us something else, and she says 'come to me' – I'm going there now."
Jule: "Yes."
Harry: "Do you want to come?"

33

Jule: "Yes."   ... ...

Harry: "The ground is a bit clayey, there are some stones in it – they are angular stones, so it's more of a mountain area, not a river valley ... the ground is dry, but not completely dry ... and it has ... something quiet, friendly."   ... ...

Harry: "Do you see anything?"

Jule: "I see their leaves in the wind ... but its a summer wind, its tender ... and the plants move."   ... ...

Harry: "Funny – I suddenly changed perspective: I'm now only two-thirds the size of a chamomile plant ... that's ... yes, an unusual perspective ..."

Jule: "That's right ... I'm looking ... I was at the same height."   ... ...

Harry: "Chamomile? Is there anything important to see here?"   ...

Chamomile: "Yourself."

Harry: "Ehm ... if I see myself, will I understand you better?"   ...

Kamille: "Try it out ..."

Harry: "Hm ... (laughs) ... I looked at myself, then I saw that I'm a chamomile plant – I hadn't noticed that before."   ... ...

Jule: "Chamomile is family ..."

Harry agrees emphatically, "Hm! ... I suddenly had the feeling I had several heads."

Jule laughs ...

Harry: "That's the flowers and multiple arms – that's all the leaves and branches ... that it feels like 'family ... ... 'Chamomile is family.' ... yes ... ... all these chamomile plants standing there, they belong together ..."

Jule: "I almost feel like they're chirping together ..."

We both laugh ...

Jule: "Like this..."

Harry: "Hm ..."   ... ...

Jule: "They are definitely quite friendly and ..."   ... ...

Harry: "Hm ... they are also sincere with each other ... sincere and full of feelings ..."

Jule: "Quite emotional – exactly."   ...

Harry: "Yes, that's the feeling of being part of 'a community ..."   ... ...

Harry (laughing with a grin): "There's something so friendly, simple about it."

Jule: "Hm."

Harry: "I just had to think of hobbits for a moment."

Jule: "Hmm."

Harry: "It's not exactly the same, but it has a resemblance." ... ...

Harry: "There's caring for each other, too."

Jule: "Hm."   ... ...

Harry: "I just asked Chamomile again if there was anything to do or if it would be good to see something in particular – but she says, 'Nah, just be there.'" ... ...

Jule: "I kind of feel like the world stops when you're lying in a camomile field like that."

Harry laughs in agreement: "Yes ..."

Jule: "There's something totally timeless about it ..."

Harry: "Do you mean that now on this dream journey or do you mean that now in real life?"

Jule: "Hm ... I mean, now, when I imagine lying down where the chamomile grows, that you can lie there like that ..."

Harry: "Hmm."

Jule: "The ... the heads nod in the wind and ... that smells so ... so nice and ... and ... that has something, where you can dream and ... daydream or ... ehm ... that has something very calm, something so ... where you can really come down ..."

Harry: "Hm ..."

Jule: "The scent has nothing overpowering at all – it's clear and ... but not oppressive – I don't find it oppressive at all ..."

Harry: "I always have to get into it first."

Jule: "To the scent of chamomile?"

Harry: "Hm ... that's okay then, but it's like ... 'Yeah, well, now I'll do that.' So ..."

Jule: "Hm ... well, I can't drink chamomile tea at all when I'm sick – well, everyone says that if you have a stomach ache or if you're sick, you should drink chamomile tea, I find that ... I could puke right away ... so that's so right for me ... that doesn't fit together at all."

Harry: "Hm ..."

Jule: "For me, it's more like ... it also has something of a closing time ..."

Harry: "Hm ..."

Jule: "And sitting together."

Harry laughs in agreement, "Yes – and having roots ..."

Jule: "Yes!" ...

Harry: "Somehow the roots are important with this chamomile, although they are not big or ... not clinging or anything, but it has something ... to have such a hold, to have such a backing, such security ..."

Jule: "Earlier I had a picture of the roots, that they touch each other ... that is, that they are underground, that the plants somehow ..."

Harry: "Hm ..."

Jule: "That they touched each other so lightly with their tips ..."

Harry: "Hm."

Jule: "Then I could get into the roots of one of them and then over there and then up there ..."

Harry laughs with a grin, enjoying himself ...

Jule: "As if the hands were holding ... You know?"
Harry: "Yeah."
Jule: "Something like that ..."
Harry: "Yeah." ... ...
Harry: "Do the root sprouts?"
Jule: "I don't think so."
Harry: "I don't think so either, actually."
Jule: "I think they're annuals ... they seed from ..." ...
Harry: "I think they feel safe in the ground ..."
Jule: "Hm."
Harry: "Well, 'they' ... I could say 'we' – I'm a chamomile plant right now, too." ...
... ...
Harry: "I feel like there's no long journeys or big experiences or transformations or anything dramatic like that here – it's just so ... like so, yeah, sitting in the nest enjoying ..."
Jule: "Hmm."
Harry: "Sitting in the nest, enjoying and secure – like that ..." ... ...
Jule: "Also something lying down, like that ... with me it's not 'nest', it's like a cradle."
Harry laughs: "Yes, 'cradle' fits even better." ... ...
Harry: "Yes, I always have the feeling that chamomile is a little children's plant."
Jule: "Hm." ... ...
Harry: "I asked the chamomile if there was anything else to see, and she said, 'You're here.' ... I also have the feeling that what I'm experiencing or feeling right now is what the chamomile is all about."
Jule: "Hm." ... ...
Harry: "Do you still want to stay there, or do you feel like it's a good thing?" ... ...
Jule: "It's good like this."
Harry: "Hm, I have that feeling, too. ... Thank you chamomile!"
Jule: "Yes - thank you!"
Harry: "Ho!" ... ...
Harry: "That is Lunar."
Jule: "Lunar?"
Harry: "Yes." ...
Jule: "Yeah, maybe that's the powerful, but coolness ... but also not cold."
Harry: "Nah, it's not cold."
Jule: "Lunar." ... ...
Harry: "I'm impressed with how different the qualities are from these plants."
Jule: "Yes ..."

Harry: "I couldn't have imagined that before." ...

Jule: "I knew it was, but I didn't ... I didn't really have any idea how ... do you know what I mean?"

Harry: "Hm ... hm, with healing stones I actually know that, I could have transferred that to the plants, but I didn't ... I like that with these different qualities ..."

VI 2. Peppermint

Harry: "Peppermint, we'd like to get to know you better. ... When I was just gearing up to ask the peppermint, I already got this feeling, like of ... yeah, I'll say, of freshness and freedom."

Jule: "Yes, cool wind."

Harry: "Hm ... ... It's as if I see someone looking around like this: 'So, what can we do now?' ... Something so enterprising ... ... Do you want to tell us or show us something, Peppermint?"

Peppermint: "I've already started." ... ...

Harry: "Peppermint – is that the reason why I can see inwardly the Ahr Valley mountains?"

Peppermint: "That's where you like it – and there's space when you're up there." ...

Harry: "Yes, that's right – that's where I like to be." ... ...

Harry: "I just heard Peppermint ask me if we wanted to go there, and I'm a bit irritated, because it's such a concrete place ... a bit west of the 'Bunte Kuh' on the north side of the Ahr ... hm ... What's going on with you, Jule?"

Jule: "Well, I saw peppermint in the water and it was very cool water, but flowing like a spring, very fresh and pure..."

Harry: "Hm .... that grew there in the water, right?"

Jule: "Yes." ...

Harry: "I think I'll come into your picture. ... Hmm ... Oh, this water has a good taste!"

Jule: "Hm."

Harry (laughing): "Peppermint water." ... ...

Harry (taking a deep breath): "I asked her if there was anything to do – and she then asked me what I wanted to do." ...

Harry: "I want to experience nice things." ...

Peppermint: "What things?" ...

Harry: "I don't know that specifically yet." ...

Peppermint: "And how could you tell that they are beautiful things?" ...

Harry: "There would be a feeling of lightness, of effortlessness ... of joy ... of being touched ... enriched ... of freshness ... hm ... I would like that." ... ...

Harry takes a deep breath. ... ...

Harry: "Ehm, peppermint – do I have to do anything for that now?" ... ...

Peppermint: "You have to wish for it ... and trust that the wish will come true." ...

Harry: "Okay, I'll do it then." ...

Harry (laughing): "A basic lesson in magic, so to speak." ... ...

Harry takes a deep breath – is this deep breathing 'pepperminty'? ... ...

Harry: "What's up with you, Jule?" ...

Jule: "I just have the feeling that the peppermint is cleaning through me."

Harry (laughing with a grin): "I can imagine that."

Jule: "Yes, that's nice!"

Harry: "I had a similar feeling just now, when I imagined and wished for all these very qualities."

Jule: "Hm." ... ...

A very long pause of two minutes; now and then a deep breath from Harry. ... ...

Harry: "Peppermint – would it be helpful if I did anything in particular if I wanted to get to know you better?" ... ...

Peppermint: "You can get to know me better by trying to live as I am – that's the most direct method." ...

Harry: "That is – this wishing and trusting that it will come true?"

Peppermint: "Yes." ...

Harry takes another deep breath ...

Harry: "Is it better to wish for something in general or to wish for something concretely?"

Peppermint: "Wish as the wish is – how else?" ...

Harry: "Yes, fine." ... ...

Another long pause of two minutes; now and then a deep breath from Harry. ... ...

Harry: "So my main feeling is that the peppermint clears paths. ... Yes, and cleanses." ...

Jule: "With me, it has now gone completely through the body and made everything somehow ... so ... all cleaned through ... so ... yes, somehow so ... ... fresh and airy." ...

Another deep breath from Harry. ... ... Another long pause of a minute; now and then a deep breath from Harry. ... ...

Harry: "Peppermint, is there anything more to discover?" ... ...

Harry: "I mean that she says there is nothing else – that she is just that." ... ...

A deep breath from Harry – all those noticeable deep breaths are through the nose, not the mouth. ...

Jule: "Just now I had the image that she was cleaning me like this ... like this and ... and at the same time she made me such little wings ... on my arms."

Harry: "Hm ... little wings – fits somehow well."

Jule: "Yes, and I had the feeling that if, if the ... I had the feeling that I could just circle like a hawk, like a bird of prey, like that, just like that, above our heads, like that, and look ..."

Harry: "Hm."

Jule: "Ah, the wings were made of their leaves."

Harry: "Hmm ... the leaves or the petals?"

Jule: "The leaves."

Harry: "Hmm."

Jule: "They were kind of like scales on top of each other."

Harry: "Hmm."

Harry takes another deep breath. ...

Harry: "That's a nice feeling, flying up there and looking down." ... ...

Harry: "I also have the feeling all the time with all the pictures I see like this, it's all sunny and bright, but it's not warm."

Jule: "Hm." ...

Harry: "Just a bright clarity like that."

Jule: "Hm." ... ...

Jule: "Where it was in the water, by the spring, it was even half-shaded, so by me."

Harry: "Hm, yes."

Jule: "There was such a very mixed light, it wasn't so ... but still very bright."

Harry: "That's how I saw it, too."

Jule: "I still saw it very ... just this very clear air and this very clear water ... er ... that was very cool and ... fresh, but totally bright ..."

Another long pause of a minute; now and then a deep breath from Harry. ... ...

Harry: "I just asked Peppermint if she wants to show me something else, and she thinks I should come with her ... she's going back towards 'Bunte Kuh', that is, to this mountain on the Ahr."

Jule: "Hm." ... ...

Harry takes a deep breath.

Harry: "I'm sitting there now ... not too far below the summit ... so on the west side and looking ... south into the Ahr valley ... and the peppermint asked me if I wouldn't like to go there, ... and somehow I think it fits ... I'm thinking about which of my flutes I would like to play here ... I think ... my bamboo flute fits best ... ... hm – it has a much higher tone than usual ..."

Jule: "I was about to say, I'd rather use the tin whistle for that – it fits so well."

Harry: "Yes, I had it in my hand for a short time, yes ... (laughs) and my bamboo transverse flute sounds almost like that now, too." ... ...

A deep breath from Harry.   ... ...

Harry: "I've stopped playing the flute now, and now I'm leaning with my back against the rock, half lying like this ... I can feel the wind and the sun ... yes ... there I am just so content ..." ... ...

Harry: "What are you experiencing?" ...

Jule: "I've just digressed."

Harry: "Hm." ...

Another deep breath from Harry.   ... .

Harry: "I actually feel like it's a good thing – I had that a while back ... I think the peppermint makes you ... kind of satisfied anyway ..."

Jule: "Hm." ...

Harry: "What do you mean – do you want to look further?"

Jule: "Nah, I'm done."

Harry: "O.k. ... yes, peppermint – thank you very much!"

Jule: "Yes, thank you!"

Peppermint: "Here you go!"

Harry: "Ho!" ... ...

We both laugh contentedly ...

Harry: "They have such a distinct character, these plants ..."

Jule: "Hm."   ... ...

Harry: "Now I suddenly have the taste of ... what is it ... there are such bars of peppermint-flavored sugar, they are half white and half pink ... such thick blocks ..."

Jule: "I don't know those – I only know those lentils ... those chocolate lentils with peppermint chocolate ... that are also pink or white."

Harry: "Yeah, when the chocolate's gone, it's the same thing."

Jule: "Yeah, okay, yeah, I can imagine that – sugar stuff like that, right?"

Harry (laughing): "Yeah."

Jule: "Oh, those chocolate lentils! I thought they were so yummy! I ate those all the time for a couple of years!"

Jule laughs.

Harry: "I'll see if I can find them somewhere – I'm in the mood for them right now!"

Jule: "Oh, me too!"

We both laugh out loud.

Jule: "Oh, we're going to buy chocolate lentils right now!"

We are still laughing ...

Harry: "Yes, I prefer those without chocolate – let's see."

40

Jule: "Yes, and 'after eight' is also so delicious – only they were bought by Nestle and I don't like them!"

VI 3.   Sage

This was Jules' first plant dream trip.

Harry: "To proceed ..."
Jule: "Hm ..."
Harry: "... so ... the way I've been doing it lately is that I just talk to the sage inside and tell it what I want ..."
Jule: "Hm ..."
Harry: "... and then I look to see if I see any images or if anything comes ..."
Jule: "Hm ..."
Harry: "... and I would just start – and if you perceive something or see something, then you can just say something. ... Well, half the time I don't say anything anyway, because I'm always listening and looking."
Jule: "Hm..."
Harry: "Shall we just see how it goes and change something if necessary?"   ...
Jule: "Yes. ... Well – with me it's still a question of how I can get there in the first place, something like that ... well ... I can imagine a sage ... er ... but I can't differentiate what I'm interpreting into it and what I really see."
Harry: "You don't need to know at the beginning. ... The first part is just pronouncing it – it doesn't matter where it comes from."
Jule: "O.k. ..."
Harry: "It's like when a chemist dumps two things together – he puts on his safety clothes, puts on his glasses and dumps them together and sees what happens."
Jule: "Hm ..."
Harry: "Then he notes how much property damage there is, how hot it got and what it stank of – and then he knows what happens when he mixes the two things and then he can think about ... but only afterwards ... that was like that ... so there is the phase when ..."
Jule: "Yes, I have, I have the feeling that I stay in the theme – that's what I mean. You know, what I ... that is ..."
Harry: "Oh, I see – can you imagine that you are dreaming about the sage, so to speak, and that you are talking to the sage in your dreams? ... Or that you are now going into a fairy tale in which the plants can speak?"   ...

41

Jule: "I can try it out... try it out..." ...

Harry: "O.K. ... Let's just do it ..."

Jule: "Yes."

Harry: "... and see what comes up."

Jule: "Yes."

Harry takes a deep breath ...

Harry: "Hi, Sage ... we'd like to get to know you better ... well, I know you as a spice, as a plant and for incense and ... I have you with me as a plant on the balcony ... and if you'd like to tell us something ... that would be nice."

Sage: "O.k., what do you want to know?"

Harry: "Well ... I don't really have anything specific I want to know – I just want to get to know you." ...

Sage: "Well, look." ...

Harry: "I'm looking." ... ...

Harry: "I see a landscape ... there are a lot of angular stones 'around' ... so probably a plateau rather than flatland ..."

Jule: "That's totally dry."

Harry: "Yeah ... there's herbs and ... yeah, so ... thorn bushes, I guess ..."

Jule: "It's very silvery."

Harry: "Mm ... It smells a bit dusty-aromatic ... it reminds me a bit of the South of France ..."

Jule: "And it's windy and warm, too."

Harry: "Yes, it's actually even drier than most areas in the south of France."

Jule: "Mm ..."

Harry: "A plateau or so."

Jule: "It reminds me a bit of – I was once in Crete – it was so stony and dry."

Harry: "That could be – I haven't been to Crete yet. What is ..."

Jule: "Although – in Crete it was mountainous and this is not mountainous."

Harry: "Nah – it's like a plain."

Jule: "Yes."

Harry: "Good. ... Sage?"

Sage: "Yeah?"

Harry: "Is there a place here that's particularly important or where we can learn about you? ... ... The sage says that I should go a little bit straight ahead, but not far. ... There's something strange on the ground. It looks like a hole, but it's not a hole. ... So ... Huh? What's that? ... about three or four meters in diameter ... it has something shiny, black, but also ... like light reflections ... what is that??? ... Do you see that, Jule?"

Jule: "No."

Harry: "Sage? What is that I see there?"

Sage: "That's my shadow."

Harry: "Your shadow? ... Huh? ... I'll sit in front of it ... ... Do I see as an image an effect of you, Sage, on people?"

Sage: "You could call it that." ...

Harry: "How can I find out what that effect is?"

Sage: "By going inside." ...

Harry: "Can I also get ... out of it without having to take that quality with me?" ...

Sage: "Yes." ...

Harry: "O.k. ... er ... would you like to come with me there, Jule?"

Jule: "Yes, I'd love to go, but I can't see it right now."

Harry: "I can just take you by the hand, then ..."

Jule: "I'll go piggyback."

Harry: "Piggyback? Yes, that's also fine for me ..."

Harry takes Jule on his back on the dream journey.

Harry: "Funny, you're totally light ..."

Jule laughs.

Harry walks with Jule piggyback into the black.

Harry: "O.k. ... oh ... that's not going in at all, that's ... that's not falling either ... that's like ... like floating ... strange ... ... Is there anything special here?" ... ...

Harry: "It's pulling something in my belly, so my solar plexus and my hara, it's pulling a little bit together ... is just ... is actually not unpleasant, it's ... feels like 'a certain form of concentration ... it's a kind of feeling ... yes, kind of sobriety ... Sage?"

Sage: "Yes?"

Harry: "Would it be conducive for me to do anything specific here? So conducive – that I can understand this?" ...

Sage: "Let that blackness into you."

Harry does. ... ...

Harry: "It reminds me of something! ... Of a dream journey I made with Jörg to Binah! To the sphere on the Tree of Life ... there, where you can find the community of all beings – we went through a long tunnel before we got there ... Does that have something to do with it, Sage?" ... ...

Sage: "Look." ... ...

Harry: "Where are you right now, Jule? Do you perceive anything?" ...

Jule: "I have the feeling that it's very dark around me, but that's all I can say." ... ...

Harry: "I see like so dimly Aztec or rather Toltec temple fronts ... What is this doing here?" ...

Sage: "Keep looking." ... ...

43

A very deep breath from Harry ... ...

Harry: "It's getting calmer inside me. ... It's like letting go and arriving. ... A little bit like in the sweat lodge." ...

Sage: "You're looking at the sage places right now."

Harry: "Hmm ... Are there more of them? ... ... I'm looking at prairie ... oddly enough, I feel like I'm smelling buffalo, even though I really have no idea what buffalo smells like ... Are these pictures the gist of it, Sage?"

Sage: "No."

Harry: "How do we find the essence?"

Harry: A very deep sigh ...

Sage: "Let go." ... ...

Harry: Another very deep sigh ... ...

Harry: "I smell sage ... the scent ... yes, somehow it's starting to fill me up ... not quite – mainly respiratory, but ... that goes beyond ... ..."

Harry: Another deep sigh ... ...

Harry: And another deep sigh ... ...

Harry: "Do you want me to keep just letting go, Sage?" ...

Sage: "What do you feel?" ...

Harry: "Calmness, serenity ... ... there's something tidy about it somehow ..."

Jule: "Tidy in the head."

Harry: "Yes. ... Things are in their place, they're not all done, but ... they're there just ..."

Jule: "... or cleaned."

Harry: "Cleaned ... yeah, huh ..." ... ...

Harry: A deep breath through the nose ... ... Another deep breath through the nose ...

Harry: "Hmm ... is that why they say sage cleanses?" ...

Sage: "You can see it ..." ... ...

Harry: Another deep breath and again conspicuously through the nose ...

Harry: "I notice the effect most clearly between the palate chakra and the third eye ... as if power is gathering there ..."

Jule: "Cold power, I think – it's cold for me." ...

Harry: "Yes ..."

Jule: "It's so fresh."

Harry: "Fresh, yeah – isn't a hot force ... What's that force doing there, Sage?" ...

Sage: "Just look." ... ...

Harry: A very deep sigh – this time through his mouth ... ...

Harry: "It connects something in me ... it gives my ideas and concepts and intentions in my third eye ... it kind of gives them roots ... it brings that like down to earth, so ... in a friendly way ... like then I can see much better ... what's actually

44

important ... yes ... ... and that reaches into the chest area ... I don't know if it's up to the heart chakra, but up into the chest area anyway ... but the main point is there under the third eye ... ..."

Harry: A rather quick and very deep breath ... ...

Harry: "I keep having to smile, I don't know why actually, but ... so ... it's like such gratuitous joy there ... somehow that comes from what the sage is doing there in the ... yes, under the third eye ... ..."

Harry: Another deep inhale through the nose, which then turns into a hearty yawn ... this 'differentiated deep breathing and sighing' has not occurred before on other dream journeys.   ... ...

Harry: "Tell me, Sage, did this rocky, dry plain have anything to do with cerebral preconceptions?"

Sage: "You better look – the question is cerebral."   ...

Harry: "Yes, good."   ... ...

Harry: "What's up with you, Jule?"

Jule: "I think this is his favorite place."

Harry: "This place?"

Jule: "Mm."   ... ...

Harry: "For me, that's where it really starts to work. ... So, a bit like something is being kneaded or pushed back and forth ... ..."

Harry: A deep breath through the nose... ...

Jule: "In your head?"

Harry: "Excuse me?"

Jule: "In your head?"

Harry: "Yes, that spot there ..."

Jule: "Yes."

Harry: "... under the third eye, in that space."

Jule: "Yes."

Harry: "There are movements to notice."

Jule. "Yes."   ... ...

Harry: Again, a very deep breath through the nose ... ...

Jule: "So to me it feels like it's all the sinuses, I'm so'n aware of my sinuses in my head ..."

Harry: "Mm."

Jule: "... everything that's in the palate and the forehead ... ehm ... of air space."

Jule: A long exhale ...

Harry: "Yes ..."   ...

Jule: "It's so very free."   ...

Harry: "In the meantime, I also notice the third eye itself ... so, this pleasant pressure that sometimes arises there in the beginning when meditating."   ... ...

Harry: Another deep breath through the nose ... ...

Harry: And another deep breath through the nose ... ...

Harry: "I feel a pulsation there – and it's exactly two heartbeats long ... so it's not the same rhythm as my heartbeat, but it's like two heartbeats (i.e., half as fast)." ... ...

Harry: A deep breath through the nose ... ...

Harry: "Do you want me to keep looking, Sage? Or can I ask you something?"

Sage: "Go ahead and ask." ...

Harry: "Is there anything ... yes ... that you might tell me or show me personally, that is, what ... is beneficial, helpful, enjoyable or something for me personally right now?" ...

Sage: "Look." ... ...

Harry: "I see a very small, blue ball of light, so it's ... tiny ... it's floating there in front of me ... so ... yes, I think at neck level ... maybe chin level ... so, yes ... I can hardly see the distance ... two, three meters maybe ... What do you want, ball of light?"

Light ball: "Look at me." ... ...

Harry: "You may be a ball of light, but you strike me as ... concentrated sage scent ... the ball is getting closer and bigger ..." ... ...

Harry: A deep breath through the mouth ...

Harry: "It's almost head-sized now, and just short of my neck and chin ... ... Do you want me to do anything, bullet?" ...

Kugel: "Depends on how brave you are."

Harry: "Ehm ... yes, well ... and if I'm brave?"

Kugel: "Then you jump into me."

Harry: "Hm ... do you want to come, Jule?" ...

Jule: "Yes."

Harry: "Piggyback again?"

Jule: "Yes, that was good." ...

Harry: "O.k. ... then I'll jump now ... ... It's quite bright here ... there's like ... yes, like high up in the air under the sky to ... float? fly? ... I don't know – I'm just up there ... I don't really know if there's any earth down there ... ..."

Harry: A deep sigh through the mouth ... ...

Harry: "It's bright here ... and it's wide ... and there's a lot of space ... ... it's a feeling like birds have, not that I have feathers on my back or anything, but like ... having wings ..."

Harry: A very deep sigh through the nose ... ...

Harry: "It's as if I've just arrived on the ground in the dark, to be in security, and here ... yes, where above all there is freedom ... ... Hm, that reminds me of the dream journey with Jörg to Chokmah, where we found this storm of light – opposite

Binah on the Tree of Life ... it's all not as violent as then, much more peaceful ... but the basic mood is the same ..."

Harry: Another open-mouthed sigh ... ...

Harry: "What's up with you, Jule?" ...

Jule: "Well, after we jumped ... well, after you jumped, jumped in ... I had a really great suction – well, 'suction' is not quite the right word, but it was like a tunnel ... when you ... when you feel like ... when the water flows out of the bathtub and there's a ... such, such a suction circle – what's that called?"

Harry: "Vortex."

Jule: "Yes, vortex – but that went up ..."

Harry: "Ah ..."

Jule: "I was in it, but I didn't feel like I was being hurled at all, I didn't feel like I was being catapulted, I felt like I was ... flying along ... but like this, a little ... very fast ..."

Harry: "Hm ..."

Jule: "And, and, er ... that I went up and it was bright, but it was not a plane, as you describe it ... when you then said, you are on a plane, then ... er, it then stopped. And then I didn't know anymore, since then I don't know anymore, I'm not anywhere."

Harry: "Mm ..."

Jule: "But it was really strong, it was just a kind of suction ... suction sounds as if I was sucked in – I just flew through it ..."

Harry: "No ... that's what I understood ... I'd also like to fly along there ... and come to you – is that okay?"

Jule: "Yes." ...

Harry: "I'm already ... ... hm ..."

Jule: "But then I kind of lost my way. You said you were on 'one level' and then ... ehm ..."

Harry: "Funny, I don't remember saying anything about a level."

Jule: "You said it was light and you were on a plane, but you were in the air."

Harry: "Oh, I see. Yes."

Jule: "At least that's what I understood." ...

Harry: "Should we ask this vortex to take us further to where it ... yes, where it originally wanted to take you?"

Jule: "Mm ... yes ..."

Harry: "Mm ..." ... ...

Harry: A very deep breath through the nose ... ...

Harry: Another deep breath through the nose ... ...

Jule: "I'm a bit ... just ... I feel distracted ..."

Harry: "What was the last thing you noticed? ... Or what did you perceive?"

Jule: "Well, it's totally bright as a flash ..."

Harry: "That's what I see, too."

Jule: "Very, very bright and, er ... but my body has felt so cold for a long time now that I keep coming back, that is, into my body, and that distracts me; I'm freezing cold, I think I have to pee ..."

Harry: "How?"

Jule: "I think I have to go to the bathroom."

Harry: "I see."

Jule: "I'll be right there."

Jule leaves.

Harry: "I know this sphere also from the Tree of Life, from Kether – from the very top, so the realm that represents God ... so, this white light, this floating in the sky, that's this realm of expansion in Chokmah ... and the dark is Binah, this security ... but that's seen from the sage ... everything is much ... gentler, milder, softer ... than when you're doing dream journeys there on the Kabbalistic Tree of Life ... It reminds me of being anointed a king, so ... sounds like 'sage' ... and a king symbolically journeys to God at his coronation ..."

Harry: A deep sigh through his nose ... ...

Jule is back from the loo.

Harry: "What is conducive to do now, Sage?" ...

Sage: "Nothing special – enjoy ..." ... ...

Harry: "When I'm in this light, then ... I just have to smile all the time because it's so pleasant." ... ...

Harry: A deep sigh through his nose ... ...

Harry: "Do you, Jule, want to ask the sage something too?" ... ...

Harry: A deep sigh through his nose ... ...

Jule: "I still have to come back in, I haven't arrived yet; I'm too fixed in the head right now."

Harry: "Do you want me to get you back there?" ... ...

Jule: "Yes." ... ...

Harry: "O.k. ... I see you now on my right ..." ... ...

Harry: A deep sigh through the nose ... ...

Harry: Another deep sigh through the nose ... ...

Jule: "I want to ask the sage something else, but I don't know what, and somehow I don't dare." ...

Harry: "Hm ... You can also just tell the sage to see what your question is and then give you the answer. Is that possible?" ...

Jule: "Yes." ... ...

Harry: A deep breath through the nose ... ...

Jule: "I kind of have the feeling that it's going back into something, something dark,

48

something high."   ...

*   Harry: "Mm ... ... should I come with you?"   ...*

*   Jule: "Yes."*

*   Harry: "O.k. ... ... If you like, you can ask where the most important thing is here."*
... ...

*   Jule: "I don't know what that has to do with it now, but I just have the feeling, kind of like a bird's nest, only bigger."*

*   Harry laughs softly to himself ...*

*   Jule: "And I'm just like that in there ... curled up, somehow."*

*   Harry: "Yeah."*

*   Jule: "That's quite comfortable."*

*   Harry: "I saw something like a nest, too; I felt like this nest – I felt like it was on the ground."*

*   Jule: "Mm, it goes into the ground a little bit ..."*

*   Harry: "Yeah."*

*   Jule: "... but not like a cave ..."*

*   Harry: "No, no, not that."*

*   Jule: "... more like a hollow in the forest or something."*

*   Harry: "And this nest, in places it has something shimmering or ... like it's glowing a bit or something ..."   ... ...*

*   Jule: "This is just a cozy place."*

*   Harry laughs quietly to himself ...*

*   Harry: "Yes, I'll sit cross-legged next to it, like this ... look how you're lying there ... I think it would fit better if I lay down there too ... ... The sage asked me if I wanted a nest too ... yes ... now I have one too ... ..."*

*   Jule: "I feel quite safe in there, it's quite cozy and quite protected."*

*   Harry: "Mm..."   ...*

*   Jule: "And so completely borne ... ... and soft ..."*

*   Harry: "Yes, it's not a nest of branches, nah ..."*

*   Jule: "It's very soft ..."*

*   Harry: "Very soft ..."*

*   Jule: "More like moss..."   ... ...*

*   Jule: "Hm ..."   ... ...*

*   Harry: "Is there anything else, Sage, that you want to show me or us?"*

*   Sage: "What else do you need?"*

*   Harry: "I don't really need anything ... but maybe there's something ... ... I have a feeling there's something else, but it's not on the agenda right now."*

*   Sage: "That's right."   ...*

*   Harry: "Yes, fine."   ...*

*   Harry: Another deep breath through his nose ... ...*

Harry: "I think I might go back now."
Jule: "Mm."
Harry: "You too?" ...
Jule: "Yes."
Harry: "O.k. Then I'll go back out of the dream journey now. ... Thank you, Sage."
Jule: "Yes, thank you."
Sage: "Here you go."
Harry: "Ho!"

English Books by Harry Eilenstein

- Living Magic (261 p.)	- Mandalas for Beginners
- The Synthesis of Physics and Magic (192 p.)	- Money Magic for Beginners
- Astral Projection for Beginners (60 p.)	- Love Magic for Beginners
- Invocations for Beginners (52 p.)	- Magic Research for Beginners
- Evocations for Beginners (62 p.)	- Self-awareness for Beginners
- Auto-Movement for Beginners (60 p.)	- Symbolism of Numbers for Beginners
- Elves for Beginners (56 p.)	- Language of the Moon – for Beginners
These books will be puplished soon:	- Magic Chant for Beginners
- Telepathy for Beginners	- Prophecy for Beginners
- Telepathy for Advanced Learners	- Shamanism for Beginners
- Telekinesis for Beginners	- Magic Objects for Beginners
- Life Force for Beginners	- Da'ath-Magic for Beginners
- Meditation for Beginners	- Crop Circles for Beginners
- Kundalini for Beginners	- Feng Shui for Beginners
- Hypnosis for Beginners	- Magic for Beginners – Anthology I
- Chakra-Magic for Beginners	- Magic for Beginners – Anthology II
- Astrology for Beginners	- Magic for Beginners – Anthology III
- Ritual Magic for Beginners	- Magic for Beginners – Anthology IV

Bücher von Harry Eilenstein

Religion allgemein	Germanen
- Die sieben Schritte des Lebens (428 S.)	- Die Götter der Germanen (87 Bände – siehe
- Muttergöttin und Schamanen (168 S.)	nächste Seite)
- Göbekli Tepe (472 S.)	- Odin (300 S.)
- Die Göttin von Göbekli Tepe (144 S.)	**Kelten**
- Totempfähle (440 S.)	- Cernunnos (690 S.)
- Christus (60 S.)	- Taliesin (228 S.)
- Dakini (80 S.)	- Der Kessel von Gundestrup (220 S.)
- Vajra (76 S.)	- Der Chiemsee-Kessel (76)
Ägypten	**Psychologie**
- Hathor und Re 1: Götter und Mythen im	- Über die Freude (100 S.)
Alten Ägypten (432 S.)	- Das Geheimnis des inneren Friedens (252 S.)
- Hathor und Re 2: Die altägyptische Religion –	- Das Beziehungsmandala (52 S.)
Ursprünge, Kult und Magie (396 S.)	- Gefühle und ihre Verwandlungen (404 S.)
- Isis (508 S.)	- einsgerichtet (140 S.)
Indogermanen	- Liebe und Eigenständigkeit (216 S.)
- Die Entwicklung der indogermanischen	- Von innerer Fülle zu äußerem Gedeihen (52 S.)
Religionen (700 S.)	**Heilung**
- Wurzeln und Zweige der indogermanischen	- Die Symbolik der Krankheiten (76 S.)
Religion (224 S.)	**Kunst**
	- Herz des Tanzes – Tanz des Herzens (160 S.)
	Drama
	- König Athelstan (104 S.)

Bücher von Harry Eilenstein

„Magie für Anfänger"

- Telepathie für Anfänger (60 S.)
- Telepathie für Fortgeschrittene (52 S.)
- Telekinese für Anfänger (52 S.)
- Lebenskraft für Anfänger (60 S.)
- Meditation für Anfänger (56 S.)
- Kundalini für Anfänger (100 S.)
- Hypnose für Anfänger (56 S.)
- Auto-Movement für Anfänger (56 S.)
- Chakra-Magie für Anfänger (148 S.)
- Astralreisen für Anfänger (56 S.)
- Astrologie für Anfänger (120 S.)
- Ritual-Magie für Anfänger (56 S.)
- Mandalas für Anfänger (68 S.)
- Geldzauber für Anfänger (56 S.)
- Liebeszauber für Anfänger (52 S.)
- Invokationen für Anfänger (52 S.)
- Evokationen für Anfänger (60 S.)
- Elfen für Anfänger (56 S.)
- Magie-Forschung für Anfänger (140 S.)
- Selbsterkenntnis für Anfänger (52 S.)
- Zahlensymbolik für Anfänger (60 S.)
- Die Sprache des Mondes – für Anfänger (116 S.)
- Zaubergesänge für Anfänger (100 S.)
- Zukunftschau für Anfänger (60 S.)
- Schamanismus für Anfänger (52 S.)
- Magische Gegenstände für Anfänger (68 S.)
- Da'ath-Magie für Anfänger (64 S.)
- Kornkreise für Anfänger (348 S.)
- Feng Shui für Anfänger (96 S.)
- Magie für Anfänger – Sammelband I (696 S.)
- Magie für Anfänger – Sammelband II (664 S.)
- Magie für Anfänger – Sammelband III (580 S.)

„Traumreisen"

- Traumreisen zu Heilpflanzen (700 S.)

Magie

- Handbuch für Zauberlehrlinge (408 S.)
- Tarot (104 S.)
- Physik und Magie (184 S.)
- Die Synthese von Physik und Magie (200S.)
- Die Magie-Formel (156 S.)
- Krafttiere – Tiergöttinnen – Tiertänze (112 S.)
- Schwitzhütten (524 S.)
- Mythen und Magie der Harfe (116 S.)
- Magie heute – Berichte aus der Praxis (288 S.)

Meditation

- Der Lebenskraftkörper (230 S.)
- Die Chakren (100 S.)
- Das Chakren-System mit den Nebenchakren (296 S.)
- Organe und Chakren (64 S.)
- Die platonischen Körper in den Chakren (156 S.)
- Meditation (140 S.)
- Drachenfeuer (124 S.)
- Kundalini I (676 S.)
- Reinkarnation (156 S.)
- einsgerichtet (140 S.)

Astrologie

- Astrologie (496 S.)
- Photo-Astrologie (428 S.)
- Die astrologischen Aspekte (88 S.)
- Horoskop und Seele (120 S.)

Kabbala

- Kursus der praktischen Kabbala (150 S.)
- Eltern der Erde (450 S.)
- Blüten des Lebensbaumes:
    - Die Struktur des kabbalistischen Lebensbaumes (370 S.)
    - Der kabbalistische Lebensbaum als Forschungshilfsmittel (580 S.)
    - Der kabbalistische Lebensbaum als spirituelle Landkarte (520 S.)

Die Themen der 87 Bände der Reihe „Die Götter der Germanen"

1. Die Entwicklung der germanischen Religion
2. Lexikon der germanischen Religion
3. Der ursprüngliche Göttervater Tyr
4. Tyr in der Unterwelt: der Schmied Wieland
5. Tyr in der Unterwelt: der Riesenkönig   Teil 1
6. Tyr in der Unterwelt: der Riesenkönig   Teil 2
7. Tyr in der Unterwelt: der Zwergenkönig
8. Der Himmelswächter Heimdall
9. Der Sommergott Baldur
10. Der Meeresgott: Ägir, Hler und Njörd
11. Der Eibengott Ullr
12. Die Zwillingsgötter Alcis
13. Der neue Göttervater Odin   Teil 1
14. Der neue Göttervater Odin   Teil 2
15. Der Fruchtbarkeitsgott Freyr
16. Der Chaos-Gott Loki
17. Der Donnergott Thor
18. Der Priestergott Hönir
19. Die Göttersöhne
20. Die unbekannteren Götter
21. Die Göttermutter Frigg
22. Die Liebesgöttin: Freya und Menglöd
23. Die Erdgöttinnen
24. Die Korngöttin Sif
25. Die Apfel-Göttin Idun
26. Die Hügelgrab-Jenseitsgöttin Hel
27. Die Meeres-Jenseitsgöttin Ran
28. Die unbekannteren Jenseitsgöttinnen
29. Die unbekannteren Göttinnen
30. Die Nornen
31. Die Walküren
32. Die Zwerge
33. Der Urriese Ymir
34. Die Riesen
35. Die Riesinnen
36. Mythologische Wesen
37. Mythologische Priester und Priesterinnen
38. Sigurd/Siegfried
39. Helden und Göttersöhne
40. Die Symbolik der Vögel und Insekten
41. Die Symbolik der Schlangen, Drachen und Ungeheuer
42.a Die Symbolik der Herdentiere I
42.b Die Symbolik der Herdentiere II
43. Die Symbolik der Raubtiere
44. Die Symbolik der Wassertiere und sonstigen Tiere
45. Die Symbolik der Pflanzen
46. Die Symbolik der Farben
47. Die Symbolik der Zahlen
48. Die Symbolik von Sonne, Mond und Sternen
49.a Das Jenseits I – Das Hügelgrab
49.b Das Jenseits II – Der Jenseitsweg
50. Seelenvogel, Utiseta und Einweihung
51. Wiederzeugung und Wiedergeburt
52. Elemente der Kosmologie
53. Der Weltenbaum
54. Die Symbolik der Himmelsrichtungen und der Jahreszeiten
55.a Mythologische Motive I
55.b Mythologische Motive II
56. Der Tempel
57. Die Einrichtung des Tempels
58. Priesterin – Seherin – Zauberin – Hexe
59. Priester – Seher – Zauberer
60. Rituelle Kleidung und Schmuck
61. Skalden und Skaldinnen
62 Kriegerinnen und Ekstase-Krieger
63. Die Symbolik der Körperteile
64.a Magie und Ritual I
64.b Magie und Ritual II
64.c Magie und Ritual III
65. Gestaltwandlungen
66.a Magische Angriffs-Waffen
66.b Magische Verteidigungs-Waffen
67. Magische Werkzeuge und Gegenstände
68. Zaubersprüche
69. Göttermet
70. Zaubertränke
71. Träume, Omen und Orakel
72. Runen
73. Sozial-religiöse Rituale
74. Weisheiten und Sprichworte
75. Kenningar
76. Rätsel
77. Die vollständige Edda des Snorri Sturluson
78. Frühe Skaldenlieder
79.a Mythologische Sagas I
79.b Mythologische Sagas II
80. Hymnen an die germanischen Götter